Eminent Reckoning!

The failure to embrace human equity
before seeking diversity.

Written by: Mr. Stephen G. Wright

ISBN: 978-0-9986462-2-0 - Paperback

⊗This paper meets the requirements of ANSI/NISO Z39.48-1992 (Permanence of Paper)

An Introduction

At the time of writing this, freedom of speech and an open discourse of ideas is still allowed in the United States. How long we will continue to enjoy these benefits remains to be seen! Not making certain people uncomfortable seems to be part of the new normal as is banning books. In other words, we are being schooled in the values of Autocracy 101.

Some people may suggest that this book is nothing more than subjective opinion. The difference between having an opinion and a professional opinion is a framework of knowledge based on experience. This book is intended to be a professional opinion, combined with critical observation. The cited sources quoted within are utilized to establish both an historical framework and current time frame to support my position. My writing is, most certainly, based upon experience within a professional vantage point. Do not misconstrue or misperceive anything that I'm speaking about. Read this work cover to cover (that is why it is short) before you make any assessment of my position!

Revisionist Animal Farm

The great George Orwell, author of my favorite descriptor of human nature, *Animal Farm*, wrote: "Four legs good – two legs bad". Spoiler alert…what about birds, or chickens or insects…and whomever? The basic concept of his work was to rather deftly point out, that as animals revolted against their "owners" and took over the farm from humans they, in time, became the same as the humans that once controlled them. They began with a unifying concept that the animal (four legs) is at least as worthy as, if not better than, the two-legged oppressor – the human. However, not all creatures on a farm, or in the world, have four legs. Birds and chickens, as example. That does create a problem for the so-called unifying cry and definition of "four legs good" now, doesn't it? So, a question for all you; do you seek justice or retribution?

Twice in 2021, and once so far in 2022, I gave a guest lecture on diversity at a university in Georgia. At the time I pointed out that a source, Fareed Zakaria of the program Global Public Square (G.P.S.) on CNN, indicated that in 1950 white folk made up 90% of the U.S. population. In 2021 that statistic appeared to be only around 59%. Everyone

4

else was quickly on a track to be the new majority over the new white minority. I drew the following graph on a white board (no pun intended):

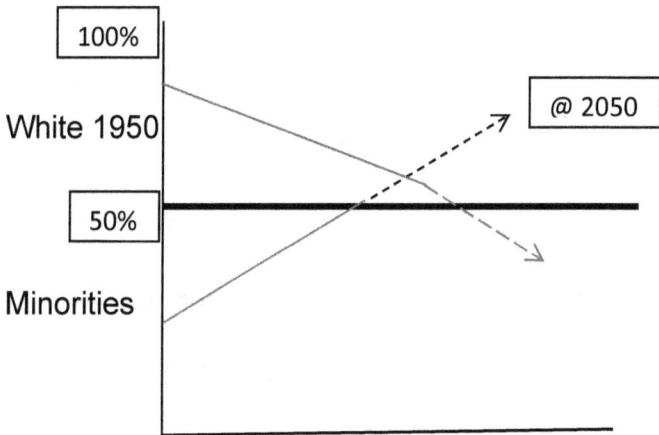

Further to this point is an article that appeared in the "*Chicago Reporter*". They indicated the following: 'By 2050 the U.S. will be a "majority-minority' country, with non-Hispanics making up less than half of the total population."[1]

When the "new minority majority" overtakes, substantially, the new "white minority", what will the consequences be? To know that the switch over has occurred, I would propose that when the House of Representatives and the Senate both are

---

[1] http://www.mikeveny.com/blog/why-employees-dont-care-about-diversity-training-html

made up of women and people of color, beyond 90%, then consideration of social realignment, and thinly vailed measures to put the oppressor in their place will not be far behind.

<u>My questions regarding the growing U.S. divide are these</u>:

- Do you want equity or control?
- At what point will diversity be reached; what is the end game?
- Is there a plan to insure equity for the new minority?

If you even begin to think, for a second, that all will be right with the world when the minority becomes majority, and we will live happily ever after you have not the slightest insight to human nature. My position is simply this - the oppressed always have a tendency toward becoming an oppressor! You forget perhaps the profusion of white anxiety on display in Charlottesville or the January 6th Trumposian insurrection? Do you really think that white folk will all breath a collective sigh of relief and say, *what a blessing, someone else is in the majority now and we can relax and let someone else do all the hard work we have done for millennia*! Is it your belief that all the oppressed people of the United States will collectively say; *Let's keep in mind how hard it was for us back then and not point fingers or place blame on those misguided, misinformed white people*! Yeah right! When teaching courses in Organizational Behavior I always ask if people are predictable? It has been my observation, both professionally and personally, that there is a degree of predictability. In my other book I stated this as Variables + Circumstances = Behavior. A cursory review of history surely illustrates the predictive nature of oppressed to oppressor behavior.

When people find power after being held back, held down, despised, ridiculed, marginalized, and dehumanized, they lash out. They scream for justice that becomes the false narrative for the truth of a divinely satisfying retribution. Yay, verily, yay – let not your anger be swayed, do unto others because they hast done such the same unto you! Think you can at least visualize more clearly now the fears being played upon and exacerbated by certain people, in certain political affiliations and in certain paramilitary and militia groups? It is these people that believe that the Anglo-Saxon message has been lost in the States. Please allow me to point out something at this point, "Anglo-Saxon values" are an ill-fitting, completely ill-assigned excuse for their own insecurity and paranoid delusional fantasy issues! Lost? A fuzzy rat's back side they lost anything! They don't seem to understand it and I doubt any of them could adequately define it.

> "In Anglo-Saxon culture and literature, to be a hero was to be a warrior. A hero had to be strong, intelligent, and courageous. Warriors had to be willing to face any odds, and fight to the death for their glory and

people. The Anglo-Saxon hero was able to be all of these and still be humble and kind. In literature Beowulf is, perhaps, the perfect example of an Anglo-Saxon hero."[2]

Without question there are those in our society that would quickly latch on to the first set of descriptors yet ignore the second. Here in lies the rub. To have Anglo-Saxon values, in the practical, operational sense, you would also need to have a balanced perspective. So, you tell me, are those yelling about the loss of Anglo-Saxon American values demonstrating humility and kindness in their words or deeds?

---

[2] https://csis.pace.edu/grendel/Proj2004A1/hero.html

I recall a fascinating concept from Arthurian legend; might for right – not might is right! Let me hear those that strike out against the current "minorities", describe how they are in lock step with Anglo-Saxon values.

Let's be direct and honest about one factor in an historical perspective. Specifically, that white men have screwed up a lot in the world, of course. Yet, it must be made clear that people of color from various "empires" or tribal groups have created human atrocities also. Please do investigate the Romans, Ottoman Empire, and Mongol Empire. Take a little time to look at crimes committed against rival ethnic tribal groups in Africa. The people of the Middle East have committed their share of human atrocities as well. The lesson is simple, yet easy to forget. Killing, torturing, humiliating, degrading, demoralizing and / or suppressing people that you find offensive in their look or conduct is okay *if* you are on the "right" side. Consider the following:

> "The end justifies the means is a phrase of Sergey Nechayev, the 19th century Russian revolutionary. It means that if a goal is morally important enough, any method of getting it is acceptable. The idea is ancient, but it was not meant to justify unnecessary cruelty. It was part of a

political   philosophy   called consequentialism."[3]

Black, white, or brown, it just does not make a real big difference in the historical context that human cruelty against each other is a means to an end. Hate and the genocide or enslavement of people because of politics or supposed peripheral physical differences is as old as the sun. Makes it right? Does this justify our collective inhumanity? **No**. This illustrates only that people find it is far easier

_____

[3]

https://simple.wikipedia.org/wiki/The_end_justifies_t he_means (expedient) to be bad rather than choosing the good in us.

Have you never heard of a slave rebellion (the movie Spartacus ring a bell)? What about an uprising against a dictator, autocrat, potentate, King, or Queen? One insidious example is the French Revolution. The suppressed "poor" overthrow the oppressive King and the cake obsessed Queen. Did the new citizen ruling class exact justice on the monarchs – perhaps. Decapitation is somewhat of a debatable instrument of justice and a messy bit of business at that. What about the aristocracy and the elites of French society? Justice or retribution? And speaking of Russian revolutionaries, consider what happened to the Tsar of Russia and his family. Consider how Stalin, or more currently, Putin may have read the position of Mr. Nechayev. History can provide numerous examples. Allow me to review another; one closer to home.

I asked the diversity class in Georgia if they had any insight as to what and where Appalachia was. Most said they did not, and a few gave a vague reference as to its location. A series of articles had been assembled for my presentation to paint a specific picture and support my intended points. The first article, by Rachel Ellen Simon, dealt with the "whitewashing" of the image and reality of people in that region. I read to the class an excerpt from an article, "*Whitewashing Reality: Diversity in Appalachia*", from The Appalachian Voice back in 2014. It detailed how in the 1800s a variety of ethnic and racial groups came into the Appalachian region of the States. Perhaps this may sound familiar to you, but the article further noted that racist laws were instituted designed to further the notion of white superiority. Have times really changed, or we playing "doomed to repeat"?

A critical question comes up here. A portion of those settling in the Appalachian region were the Irish. People from Ireland are, correct me if I'm wrong, white people. So, why would that region seek to enact laws that furthered racism? Simple answer. During the timeframe established in the article, Irish immigrants were thrown into the same category as black people, and the indigenous people of America. That category was "colored people".

The Irish were previously considered to be colored? That is truly fascinating! My Mother's side of the family were Irish immigrants that initially came over during the potato famine. Does this lineage hence qualify me as being a person of color? So, which kind of color am I, or you, for that matter? Think about it for a moment. What color am I, *really*? You just aren't white, or black, or yellow, or red. I offered my audience a more scientific explanation.

> "Human skin color is quite variable around the world. It ranges from a very dark brown among some Africans, Australian Aborigines, and Melanesians to a near yellowish pink among some Northern Europeans. There are no people who actually have true black, white, red, or yellow skin. These are commonly used color terms that do not reflect biological reality.

Skin color is due primarily to the presence of a pigment called melanin, which is controlled by at least 6 genes. Both light and dark-complexioned people have melanin."[4]

So, all the "white" folk are actually yellowish pink. Having recited to the class the above information, I went on to discuss the purpose of the pigmentation. Melanin reacts to UV light, and it is a filter of sorts. Those that lived in equatorial areas were darker than their Scandinavian brothers and sisters. Well, that was very accurate until humans decided to

---

[4] https://www2.palomar.edu/anthro/adapt/adapt_4.htm

pick up and check out how green the grass is on the other side of the fence.

At this juncture I took my audience back to the question of the Irish. Let's point out that they are from "Erin" and some may say Greater Scotia, to show some respect, as is their due. From a history of the immigrants from Ireland, I read the explanation of how many of them got here.

> "Herded like livestock in dark, cramped quarters, the Irish passengers lacked sufficient food and clean water. They choked on fetid air. They were showered by excrement and vomit. Each adult was apportioned just 18 inches of bed space—children half that.

Disease and death clung to the rancid vessels like barnacles, and nearly a quarter of the 85,000 passengers who sailed to North America aboard the aptly nicknamed "coffin ships" in 1847 never reached their destinations. Their bodies were wrapped in cloths, weighed down with stones and tossed overboard to sleep forever on the bed of the ocean floor.

Although most certainly tired and poor, the Irish did not arrive in America yearning to breathe free; they merely hungered to eat. Largely destitute, many exiles could progress no farther than within walking distance of the city docks where they disembarked. While some had spent all of their meager savings to pay for passage across the Atlantic, others had their voyages funded by British landlords who found it a cheaper solution to dispatch their tenants to another continent, rather than pay for their charity at home."[5]

I wonder if you may find any correlation to any other group(s) coming to our borders? Does this not sound vaguely familiar to the plight of Africans, only without the shackles? What about migrants from Central or South America? You know, all those people flooding our Southern border and "polluting" the purity of the Anglo-Saxon race. Everyone in this nation is immigrant, chowder head! As stated at the outset, you are welcome to disagree with

---

[5] https://www.history.com/news/when-america-despised-the-irish-the-19th-centurys-refugee-crisis

my view, but do not take exception to historical facts. From the same article, a few more observations from the author:

> "And in the opinion of many Americans, those British landlords were not sending their best people."

> "These people were not only poor, unskilled refugees huddled in rickety tenements. Even worse, they were Catholic."

> "Anti-Catholic, anti-Irish mobs in Philadelphia destroyed houses and torched churches in the deadly Bible Riots of 1844."[6]

---

[6] https://www.history.com/news/when-america-despised-the-irish-the-19th-centurys-refugee-crisis

Do these statements also remind us of something once expressed, much more recently, within the world of the intellectually challenged?

At this point we think back on our history, recent and otherwise, and wonder how the Irish in the States could have turned out to be such "nice" people if they had been despised "colored" folk back then? Allow me to point out something that also is a strong correlation to recent events in the voting trends in the States, and the subsequent white backlash.

"Although stereotyped as ignorant bogtrotters loyal only to the pope and ill-suited for democracy, and only recently given political rights by the British in their former home after centuries of denial, the Irish were deeply engaged in the political process in their new home. They voted in higher proportions than other ethnic groups. Their sheer numbers helped to propel William R. Grace to become the first Irish-Catholic mayor of New York City in 1880 and Hugh O'Brien the first Irish-Catholic mayor of Boston four years later."[7]

May I also make mention of the social

uproar, about the potential of a Catholic being

---

[7] https://www.history.com/news/when-america-despised-the-irish-the-19th-centurys-refugee-crisis

elected to the White House? This reference is not of President Biden it is of President Kennedy. Do a little homework and you will find that John Kennedy had a very difficult uphill battle dealing with the fact that it was widely believed that a Catholic in the White House would equate to the Pope in the White House. Kennedy was the first person of Irish-Catholic heritage to be President in the United States.

In my humble view it is a human responsibility and point of dignity that as your "label" grows in, shall we say – market share, of social recognition that you turn around to see who there may be behind you reaching up for your help. Identify for me which minority / majority groups have stood up and screamed, *justice for us and oh, by the way don't forget the indigenous people of our nation…they suffer just as we do, maybe more*! Our nation struggles to recognize and reconcile issues of racism, misogyny, greed, etc. etc. But what have white people and any minority labels done to address attempted genocide? Is the appointment of Ms. Deb Haaland, a member of the Pueblo of Laguna, to U.S. Secretary of the Interior sufficient? It is a good start, but hardly a sufficient act to make things right. Citizens of the States actively worked to wipe out the native tribes through forced relocation and slaughter but more importantly brought, from one shore across to the other, diseases never before found on this continent and was responsible for extraordinary numbers of Indian deaths. Our culture seems highly selective in its memory of history to the point of being mindless of our true history. In fact, there are many people creating revisionist history today so that difficult topics, such as slavery or indigenous genocide, need not bother us. So thoughtful of those white folks, truly thoughtful!

The degree of disadvantage faced by Indian tribes today is staggering. An article, posted in 2019, and updated in November of 2020 by PowWows.com is very reveling as to the current state of issues facing Native Americans. It reviews the extent of the challenges, at numerous levels, faced by the 567 tribes that our government officially recognizes. The article indicates that the number of issues faced by them has not been diminished over time. My recommendation is that you go to powwows.com and read the article for yourself and further, try to be of support to them. The article in question is: *Issues and Problems Facing Native Americans Today.* Many citizens of the States would find it something of an eye opener. Sad that anyone would still see this well documented historical travesty as eye opening.

Here is an interesting story from when I lived in Florida. My work brought me into contact with the Sheriff of the Seminole tribe near Lake Okeechobee. I asked him why they had a fence surrounding the entire area of the Seminole people? He looked at me and smiled, then he leaned forward and told me, "The fence is not there to keep us in…it is there to keep you out!" All the Native people of this continent deserve to be supported more vigorously and with greater respect. It is my view that they alone have a right to claim cultural independence from the U.S. society, if they wish to do so. They more than anyone have the right to speak the language of their tribe and to promote among themselves an appreciation for the customs and way of life they consider their own, to whatever extent they wish. They need not be "American" if they wish not to be. Their home and way of life was here long before us immigrants. All those others that came to these shores to build a life came here to be American and as such should all view themselves as from the States, not hyphenations!

Our nation seems to continue to flounder in the morass of bias, discrimination, and self-indulgent superiority complexes. It works both ways people! I'm curious, can white people comprehend and appreciate discrimination if they have never experienced it? I've been told they cannot. It could be believed that simply because I'm not a minority (actually, by definition, I am – I'm hearing impaired – so I am disabled) and not having had your exact same life experience I cannot understand who or what you are as a group of humans. Well in my experience I'd tell you to shut up and get a more globalized life. Just step outside the U.S. and live in other countries and <u>everyone</u>, of any race or ethnic background from the States becomes fair game for discrimination! The reason is simple, to them you are *all* a bunch of sheltered, rich, ill informed, egocentric, status obsessed Americans. Reality is not at play here – only perception. There are a lot of countries you can go to where they discriminate against you in terms of housing, pay, opportunity, inclusion (lack of) and service in shops or stores. I have lived in eight nations and have directly faced each form of discrimination just mentioned.

What could be a reason for our rather myopic view of ourselves and diversity? Could it be the fact that we are hyphenating ourselves right down the crapper! Here is a little news for you hot shot, you are about as Polish, Italian, African, Korean, Irish, English or whomever, as I am. You and I are all North Americans, from the States. We look like people from the States, walk like people from the States, gesture like people from the States and smell like people from the States. If you were born in the States, educated here, you therefore are enculturated here. If you wish to correct me by saying you are only demonstrating respect and appreciation for your heritage; I'd say you are being blind to the separatist, stratification generating environment that is brought by your little word games. *We are all from the States! Why in hell is that not sufficient for you*? Learning about your heritage is not the issue. Of course, you should be free to investigate where your great, great Grandparents came from. The issue is that when you start to try and mimic that cultural group and align yourself with a way of life that is not yours to take hold of you look a little foolish to that cultural group! We need to find more common bonds – not less.

Allow me to tell you another story from my life, in a galaxy far, far away, Washington, DC. I was invited to a party by some friends. The husband was African, and the wife was white, and from the States. I became acquainted with them while I was an adjunct at the Johns Hopkins University campus, in D.C. They were both employed "inside the Beltway". Almost all of the people at the party were African – no, not African-American, they were, you know, from the continent of Africa. Except, of course, for me, and a hand full of white folk. One young white guy, that worked in the Executive Branch, was sitting across from me on a couch. He went on and on about how brilliant Ms. Hillary Clinton was to have written "*It Takes a Village*". Others in the room were politely listening, if not politely trying to ignore him. Finally, I reached my limit. I spoke up and explained, in a firm way, that you cannot simply co-opt a specific cultural concept endemic to another cultural group, throw it into the States and expect it to be relevant! We are a society that is highly individualistic, and we are very prone to litigation. It won't work here at any time – in any way! If you went outside your home and tried to discipline the child of a neighbor, for any reason, you could get yourself sued by the neighbor or you may even get arrested. At the very least you would be told to mind your own business.

At this point, an African gentleman sitting just across from me jumped up, threw his arms in the air and yelled, "finally someone that understands!" Later he approached me and whispered – "Why do your people call themselves that?" I immediately understood what he was stating, not so much asking. Do you?

1) My "people" were fellow citizens from the States. He saw "African-Americans" as

Americans in the same way he viewed me as from this country, not from his. Hence the phrase "your people".

2) People from the States are, as pointed out before, not African in the sense of having direct, life-long, contact to the culture, norms, and values of the varied African people. Can you ever acquire some level of all these elements? Yes, to a very specific and limited degree (discussed more in my other book).

Having told this story to the diversity class in Georgia one black student stated that many people in Africa do not get along and hate each other. My response was that yes, I do know that and there are people in numerous world regions that hate each other as well. However, we desperately need to face ourselves now and work through the issues that we face, from a humanist perspective, before trying to be comparative in our value to the world.

People also need to be aware that diversity is not just about specific groups or framed to be taught to specific groups. Diversity is about *everyone* and it is for *everyone*! The value of diversity can only be found in the broadest view possible. If diversity becomes an application of tokenism based on labels, then it is only another form of racism. That is why I asked the students if they had any knowledge of Appalachia. They were also asked if they could tell me about Indian tribes in the States; could they name any of the indigenous groups of the U.S.? This is important because in Appalachia, and numerous other areas of this country, there are certainly white folks that are desperately poor that never have known "white privilege". For those that live on Indian lands their legacy is not just poverty, but also the memory of the fact as mentioned that, as a nation we tried, consciously and unconsciously, to commit genocide.

Could there be some other reason for this hyphenating schtick we're doing? I further explained to the class that humans love to group. Humans are herd animals, plain and simple! So, people with similar interests, or characteristics will generally be drawn to each other for the opportunity to have a shared experience.

At this juncture you may wish to challenge me, "Okay if you are so smart what do you suggest we do?" The analogy I've used to express my suggestion was to frame the issue, and your mind, to that of a Club House. As example, people that are short, medium, tall, they like to hang together because they share a similar attribute, height. So, they get together and create a club house where each separate type can meet, have a drink, and discuss how great it is for them to all be short, medium or tall. The problem is this – each group has a big wooden or metal door on their club and anyone outside cannot see in. Why would we want them to? After all, ***they*** are not us, ***they*** are them! Nobody likes "them" … right? Let's try this instead: take the solid door off, replace it with a screen door. You still have your club chuck full of the "us" crowd, but people outside can look in. The "them" crowd can see inside, and you can see the "thems" outside wondering what you "us" people are doing. Now, you walk up to the door and ask "them" to come in and visit. They in turn, hopefully, will invite you to their club too. The clubs may be on opposite sides of the street but...*they are all on the same damn street*! This is not so very hard to comprehend, honest!! Go ahead and have your group if you must, but don't shut others out. You could even hand out honorary memberships in the white group, Irish group, Italian group, black group, Polish group, Latino group...etc. etc. Hey people! – this is a matter of **a choice**, just as simple as that. Make the choice to allow others to get to know what you value, what you experience, what you fear (even if it is "them" you fear), what you aspire to and most importantly point out what you find interesting about the "us" or "them" group. A simple sharing of yourself with others will bring about the discovery of things you actually do share!

Done it before – do it again!

Could anything I suggest be a realistic possibility? Truth is, <u>it has already been done and it succeeded</u>. The main problem is the extraordinarily short historical memory of the people in the States. Many of us view an historical context of a few weeks or perhaps months. Makes our perspective a horribly short-sighted one at that.

A movie about this success of race relations is called "The Best of Enemies". It details the story of Ms. Ann Atwater, a black community activist and Mr. Claiborne Paul Ellis, a white supremacist.

"The movie, which tells the story of the unlikely friendship that developed between Atwater and C.P. Ellis, a local Klan leader, focuses on a 10-day "charrette," a community meeting that was organized in 1971 to grapple with the issue of school desegregation.

Atwater was selected as co-chair. The other co-chair selected was C.P. Ellis, an exalted cyclops of the local Ku Klux Klan in Durham. Atwater and Ellis hated each other."[8]

So, put the following French term, "En Charrette", in your mind and hold on to it. It means, "In the Cart". In effect a group of people are sequestered to focus efforts

---

[8]

https://www.washingtonpost.com/history/2019/04/05/ann-atwaters-amazing-rise-poverty-teen-pregnancy-best-enemies-stardom/

towards resolving or reconciling problems. This Klan member, and the black community activist were made co-chairs of a committee to reconcile the issues of school desegregation and arrive at a solution. What came out of this forced 10-day working relationship was indeed astounding. When they came close to the end of the charrette, they realized that the <u>core issue</u> was education for young people and was not an issue about white or black. They discovered something they shared, and both felt was important. At the conclusion of the charrette Mr. Ellis ripped his Klan membership card up, right in front of the crowd. Ms. Atwater and Mr. Ellis remained friends from that point forward. In my opinion, what has been done before can be done again. A charrette is, in essence, a <u>positive</u> use of the second variation of my human forecasting model, you will read about in a few pages: *If you limit the variables, control the circumstances - you can more readily influence or create behavior.* The only question is one of having the will to accept what and who we are in reality, not in perception!

Now that we have ascended the stairs of historical relevancy, we need to return to the story of the Irish immigrant and bring that to an even finer point.

> "No longer embedded on the lowest rung of American society, the Irish unfortunately gained acceptance in the mainstream by dishing out the same bigotry toward newcomers that they had experienced. County Cork native and Workingmen's Party leader Denis Kearney, for example, closed his speeches to American laborers with his rhetorical signature: "Whatever happens, the Chinese must go."
>
> Kearney and the other Irish failed to learn the lesson of their own story. Yes, the Irish transformed the United States, just as the United States transformed

the Irish. But the worst fears of the nativists were not fulfilled."[9]

Racism, bigotry and simple blind hatred of "those" people are not a point of physical appearance, vocal characteristics or lifestyle. It is a choice that you make that, most likely, is not founded in fact but on perception. Challenging your perceptions is hard!

---

[9] https://www.history.com/news/when-america-despised-the-irish-the-19th-centurys-refugee-crisis

"White Christian Nationalism"

You need a reality check!

We are pretentious in our assessment of religion and ourselves. We create images of Jesus that are incongruitous to some historical realities. Visualize once again please the rally in Charlottesville, Virginia. Rather ironic in the extreme. Here there are a group of white people stomping around with torches and screaming "Jews will not replace us". Now, I'm sure that all those people consider themselves to be upstanding, outstanding, down right up-right Christians. They go to Church on Sunday, and they pray for the redemption of their immortal souls. So that, when they die, they can go to heaven and meet......a very nice Jewish man! I'd love to hear how you intend to reconcile that little bit of historical fact when you get face-to-face with him. He will have some REALLY interesting questions for you!

Jesus is often portrayed, for some stupid reason, as being a white guy with long hair. Some of your fundamentalist, evangelical types are in for a shock, because people in the Middle East region are not as white as Jesus has been portrayed. I spent several years in the Middle East (UAE, Bahrain and Jordan) and what I am saying is based in part upon my direct observation and interactions! So, he is Jewish and from the Middle East. Based on historical record, with comparison to people in the region now, can we extrapolate, even a little? A dark or olive skin tone of Jesus could be more realistic for that region. What did I tell you about Melanin? Also, given the propensity for small creepy-crawling-bug-a-boos in that area, I also doubt long hair was the look of the day. Here again, my thought is that we create our deities to look the way **we wish** they could, would, or should look. Consider please the following:

"The long-haired, bearded image of Jesus that emerged beginning in the fourth century A.D. was influenced heavily by representations of Greek and Roman gods, particularly the all-powerful Greek god Zeus. At that point, Jesus started to appear in a long robe, seated on a throne (such as in the fifth-century mosaic on the altar of the Santa Pudenziana church in Rome), sometimes with a halo surrounding his head."

"Of course, not all images of Jesus conform to the dominant image of him portrayed in Western art. In fact, many different cultures around the world have depicted him, visually at least, as one of their own. "Cultures tend to portray prominent religious figures to look like the dominant racial identity…"

"Based on archaeological artifacts, texts, and preserved human remains, researchers can infer these traits about Jesus's physical appearance:

1. 5 Feet 5 Inched Tall
2. Brown Eyes
3. Black Hair
4. Olive-Brown Skin
5. Short Hair
6. Trimmed Beard

Since Jesus was a carpenter and walked around a lot, we can infer he was skinny and muscular. In the Gospels, Jesus also stated he didn't want to wear two tunics. So it's most likely he wore a simple tunic, to blend into Galilee's villages as a simple man."

"In 2001, medical artist Richard Neave — along with a team of Israeli and British forensic anthropologists and computer programmers — created a new image of Jesus, based on the typical 1st century, Palestinian Jewish features:

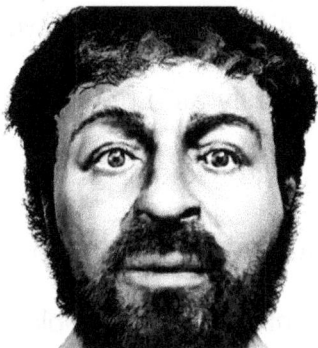

Neave and His Team's Portrayal of Jesus. Source: BBC News

With all the new evidence available, this picture is a lot more accurate to Jesus's physical appearance."[10]

"Still, at the same time, we will never know what Jesus really looked like. However, it's safe to assume that the classical portrayals of him are now outdated."[11]

---

[10] https://www.history.com/news/what-did-jesus-look-like

[11] https://historyofyesterday.com/what-did-jesus-look-like-4921eaba3cc7

So, not only is Jesus Jewish, but does he not also qualify as a person of color? This should constitute two strikes against a "White Supremacist" concept. I have heard many of my fellow humans refer to people in the Middle East as "towel heads" and other odd derogatory words and phrases. Better be careful with that, it could come back to bite you in the butt! It is not wholly impossible that Jesus wore a head covering of some form.

We humans are prone to arrogant self-indulgence without stopping to apply a dab of critical thought. Oh, excuse me, I seem to have forgotten that questions of religion are matters of faith and asking questions is usually frowned upon. Why they call it faith, right?

Would we not all be better off learning from the person he presented himself to be instead of the myth we create? Seeking historical accuracy about religious doctrine is not an act of challenging the "faith". Historical theology, and science only serve to enhance faith through clarity and reality. Where is it written that you cannot seek truth over myth?

My goal in all things is to encourage people to not be afraid to think and wonder if there could be other ways of seeing things. To discover answers and greater enlightenment. Why is this important? Because, such things should always be up for discussion, reassessment and perhaps then replacement or reacceptance.

A few predictions.

Okay, so where does all this leave us? It brings us, as I see it, right back to the beginning. You will recall I started out being down on the animal farm. It was proposed that those once oppressed, often become an oppressor.

As the number of former minority groups move into the new majority, in a more obviously visual way, and white people (read white men mostly) become the dinosaurs, the crossing of the lines is a flash point. Two things could happen:

1) A continuation of the suppression of voting rights, and thereby nullifying groups of votes, is intended to insure the election of certain types of people. As you saw previously, the key to Irish success was the ballot box. Yet, if that option is taken away, what is the logical avenue for the oppressed? Those without options, take what they perceive to be their rights. When the work of the Founding Fathers; the belief in a reasonable, thoughtful redress of grievances, is trashed what is grabbed a hold of is taking it to the streets. I do not speak of protests in the 1960s sense. Though that has been suggested as the very thing we

need. Angry people seek to vent through retribution, as was previously illustrated. Just as there are, most obviously, groups on all sides of the political spectrum, anyone perceiving they are oppressed shall begin to organize in their own defense. Or more appropriately their righteous cause of liberation from those that oppress. After all, who really has the numbers here? The oppressed or the oppressor? This is a factor that demands close consideration as perception is the thing that often rules one's judgement.

2) People with power always seek to protect the sanctity of their way of life. No, I do not see the existence of a new Civil War as it was played out before where States squared off in an attempt at establishing a new nation. A more plausible picture is to see protracted regional, local, skirmishes between armed factions. This will escalate until one side is able to inflict the greatest degree of harm to the other so that capitulation is the result. A truce, a cease fire? No, if I read the tea leaves correctly, there is a rise in tensions between us that is explosive in a devastating way. This

could be a ... be us or die moment for either side.

As indicated in the beginning of this work, I believe in what I wrote in my first book, *Reasoned Globality*. If you identify the environmental <u>variables</u> and the <u>circumstances</u> under which they exist, you are better able to predict <u>behavior</u>. V + C = B. There is a second application of this equation: If you *limit* the variables, *control* the circumstances - you can more readily *influence or create* behavior. It is this human forecasting model, the latter application, utilized *<u>in the negative context</u>*, not the former, that I see growing day-by-day. Everyone wants to control behavior instead of the more logical expression of controlling the environment. Never try to control the people! It is only ethical to control what environmental conditions surround people, while allowing them to freely exercise choice.

Is this dark, portent of doom and gloom avoidable? All things depend on the variables, and the circumstances. If you *change the environment, you change the behavior*!

Recently, I heard a political commentator reflecting on recent events as a factor of the people of the United States not truly caring about what is happening around them now. I agree with this assessment. What we face is so different, in some ways, as to be unfathomable to the American psyche on a number of levels. I'll put it this way; *we hold these truths to be.....inevitable and unchangeable?* Wrong! They are not inevitable, nor are they unchangeable! I remember something Mahatma Gandhi once expressed, "To believe in something, and not to live it, is dishonest."[12] We are not being

---

[12] https://www.goodreads.com/quotes/8052-to-believe-in-something-and-not-to-live-it-is

realistic with ourselves and certainly not honest with each other. Diversity is not just about artificial labels we create out of convenience. Diversity must, and is, by its core application, a broad-spectrum view of humanity that excludes no one. For to do so is to create divisionist, self-gratifying word play without substance. People so often create and participate in "diversity awareness" programs for the sole purpose of checking off a box that signifies they are now relevant to the society's perceptions of correctness. It is my most fervent belief that the people of this nation can self-correct and rise above the pettiness and frivolous base human emotions that have brought us to the precipice.

One person one vote. This is a simple concept and should be sacrosanct to this nation! We are marching, not walking, towards potential self-destruction. Each side has its flags raised, each side has it's rallying slogans, but not the human decency to respect our shared humanity and the brilliant foundations provided by those that created this Republic. They were not perfect by a long shot. But we must agree on some core principles that will stand the test of inevitable human idiocy. I see us as having lost our way, without just cause to be lost. One possible answer could be seen, perhaps, in the words of the "Atlas of Independence", John Adams, who said "There are only two creatures of value on the face of the earth: those with the commitment, and those that require the commitment of others". I like to combine that thought with something expressed by the late Sen. John McCain, "There is nothing more noble than serving a cause greater than yourself". Current affairs are the affairs of self-indulgence and the corruption of our national identity. This nation has never been invincible, just damn lucky and your luck, internally and internationally, is running out!

Reframe your thinking!

As I once wrote and have said in many places; how we are the same is the foundation of relationship, how we are different is the opportunity for learning. If you want to truly understand and achieve diversity you must first understand the simple truths of our shared humanity! People from all corners of the Earth seek one thing that defines a unified sense of purpose and existence ----------------------

Common Human Dignity!

Human Equity, according to Trevor Wilson, author of _Diversity at Work, The Business Case for Equity_ and president of TWI Inc.

"Human equity is about looking at a person as a whole – not their physical features, cultural background and work experience, but how all the elements of their personality work together. How is this individual greater than the sum total of their parts?"

Source: https://www.hcamag.com/ca/news/general/human-equity-moving-beyond-diversity/125188

About the Author

Mr. Wright has been actively involved in higher education, consulting, training, and public speaking throughout his rather global centric career.

Since September of 2017 he has been teaching in Georgia. Previously, he was an Assistant Professor of Management with New York Institute of Technology and a Curriculum Design Consultant for the Business Development Center in Amman, Jordan. From 2003 to 2004 he was a Visiting International Professor of Organizational Behavior and Entrepreneurship with the "Education Network

Academy", a USAID funded project, in Kazakhstan and Uzbekistan. While in Kazakhstan numerous articles regarding expatriate / local resident relations were written for the *Kazakhstan Monitor* and *Almaty Herald* newspapers and two articles for the American Chamber of Commerce.

He has worked in eight nations, within three regions of the world. Some time was also spent based in Washington, DC with international and US-based clients. During this period, the "Practical Applications in Global Business" certificate program was created and managed for George Washington University.

He is also proud of having been an adjunct member of the MBA faculty at Johns Hopkins University, teaching Managerial Communications, Global Strategic Management, Transnationalism, and Cross-cultural Management.

He was asked, in 2017, by The Atlanta Chapter of the Association for Talent Development to be a guest speaker at the meeting of the Human Capital Community of Practice. His talk was on how to effectively reconcile cross-border management issues.

Other Books by Stephen G. Wright

"*Reasoned Globality, New Organizational Pathways for International Professionals*".

This is based on teaching, research, observations, and interactions with professionals in the U.S. and abroad. The book seeks to redefine the perceptions we hold of human interactions and relationships within organizations and beyond.

Whispers from a time.

A collection of poetry written by Mr. Wright beginning in 1975. The poems cover a wide range of topics, yet focus, for the most part on love, relationships, and how we deal with life.

Contact Mr. Wright

Email: proftype@live.com

Web Site: www.reasonedglobality.com

www.ingramcontent.com/pod-product-compliance
Lightning Source LLC
Chambersburg PA
CBHW071121030426
42336CB00013BA/2160